GECKOS

ASHLEY GISH

REPTILES X BOOKS

CREATIVE EDUCATION · CREATIVE PAPERBACKS

Published by Creative Education and Creative Paperbacks · P.O. Box 227, Mankato, Minnesota 56002 · Creative Education and Creative Paperbacks are imprints of The Creative Company · www.thecreativecompany.us · Design by Rita Marshall · Production by Dana Cheit · Printed in the United States of America · Photographs by Alamy (Alan Tunnicliffe), Creative Commons Wikimedia (Robert Fisher/USGS, Alejandro Sánchez), freeVectorMaps.com, iStockphoto (ANDREYGUDKOV, jamcgraw, NNehring, PetlinDmitry, Kaan Sezer, swisshippo, visual7), Shutterstock (Robert Eastman, Stephen Marques, Nyvlt-art, Jitlada Panwiset, RealityImages, reptiles4all, Dennis van de Water, Vladimir Wrangel, Milan Zygmunt)

Library of Congress Cataloging-in-Publication Data • Names: Gish, Ashley, author. • Title: Geckos / Ashley Gish. • Series: X-Books: Reptiles. • Includes bibliographical references and index. • A countdown of five of the most fascinating geckos provides thrills as readers learn about the biological, social, and hunting characteristics of these noisy, tail-shedding reptiles. • Identifiers: ISBN 978-1-64026-081-8 (hardcover) • ISBN 978-1-62832-669-7 (pbk) • ISBN 978-1-64000-197-8 (eBook) • This title has been submitted for CIP processing under LCCN 2018939094. • CCSS: RI.3.1-8; RI.4.1-5, 7; RI.5.1-3, 8; RI.6.1-2, 4, 7; RH.6-8.3-8
First Edition HC 9 8 7 6 5 4 3 2 1 • First Edition PBK 9 8 7 6 5 4 3 2 1

GECKOS

CONTENTS

XCEPTIONAL REPTILES

Geckos are colorful creatures. Some live on the ground. Others live in trees. Special toes help them climb. Many lack eyelids. Geckos seem quiet and gentle. But they are skilled hunters.

Gecko Basics

Geckos are **reptiles**. But they do not have scales. Their skin is soft and bumpy. Like all reptiles, geckos rely on their surroundings to control their body temperature. One source of warmth is from the sun.

Many geckos have large eyes. Clear scales called brilles protect their eyes. Geckos lick their eyes to clean them.

As geckos grow, they shed their skin. Old, dry skin falls off every two to four weeks. This reveals new skin. Shedding is a natural part of gecko growth. It helps them get rid of **parasites**.

WORLDWIDE GECKOS

Geckos live on every ccntinent except Antarctica.

There are more than 1,500 different kinds of geckos.

DAY GECKOS

Day geckos are brighter colors

than those that are active at night.

NEW CALEDONIAN GECKOS

New Caledonian geckos are about 14 inches (35.6 cm) long.

They weigh less than a pound (1.6 kg).

HOUSE GECKOS

House geckos often find their way indoors.

FISH-SCALE GECKOS

Fish-scale geckos are found on Madagascar and the islands of Comoros.

JARAGUA DWARF GECKOS

Jaragua dwarf geckos grow up to 0.7 inch (1.8 cm) long. They weigh less than a single M&M® candy.

Reptiles are usually active during the day. But many geckos hunt at night. Geckos eat insects and spiders. Some also eat fruit.

TINY TEETH

Geckos have short, crooked teeth.

A gecko can walk upside down without falling. Gecko feet have tiny hairlike structures called setae. These help the gecko's feet "stick" to surfaces. In fact, a gecko needs just one toe touching the ceiling to keep it from falling. Its feet can cling to a surface even if the gecko is dead! But a gecko's feet are not sticky. Tiny **particles** called electrons are on the gecko's feet. These cling to electrons on other surfaces. This creates a strong bond. A gecko can climb just about anything!

Water bounces off gecko skin.

WATER-RESISTANT X GECKOS

GECKO BASICS FACT

Geckos active during the day have round pupils.

Nocturnal geckos have slit-shaped pupils.

TOP FIVE XTREME GECKOS

Xtreme Gecko #5

Gecko Adhesive Stanford University researchers were inspired by geckos' feet. They teamed up with NASA to make a gripping pad. They used tiny fibers that work like setae. When pressed against a surface, the pads stick! The team is hoping to use these pads to clean up space garbage. The pads could also be used to help robots make repairs on the outside of the International Space Station.

Geckos' feet cannot grip very wet or nonstick surfaces.

Gecko Babies

Geckos do not have a specific mating season. Mating is affected by weather and temperature. Some female geckos do not need males to reproduce. Instead, they produce copies of themselves! These babies are always female. Other female geckos need males to reproduce. Their babies can be male or female.

Most geckos lay eggs after mating. Females hide their eggs in dirt and leaves. Sometimes they watch over the eggs. Gecko eggs hatch in 6 to 12 weeks. The babies break through the thin shells. They are called hatchlings.

Some geckos do not lay their eggs. The mother geckos carry the eggs inside their bodies. The babies grow until they are fully developed. Then they are pushed out.

Baby geckos look like tiny versions of their parents. They can care for themselves right away. Many eat part of their egg. After about three days, they shed their skin for the first time. Then they begin to hunt. When they are about one year old, geckos search for their own mates.

1 or 2 eggs

Mother geckos lay eggs

The eggs hatch

35 to 110 days

3 to 5 days
Shed skin for the first time

up to 4 inches (10.2 cm) in length
Begin to hunt

1 to 2 years
Reproduce

GECKO BABIES FACT

Warm-weather geckos can reproduce several times per year.

Geckos in cooler places reproduce only once per year.

TOP FIVE XTREME GECKOS

Xtreme Gecko #4

Striped Gecko New Guinea's bumblebee gecko was discovered on Manus Island in 2010. This gecko has long, slender toes. Most slender-toed geckos are brown. But the bumblebee gecko sports bright yellow stripes. Only one other slender-toed gecko has lighter cclored markings. Australia's black mountain gecko has grayish-blue bands. Scientists believe these geckos developed their coloring to hide in their forest floor homes.

XTRAORDINARY LIFESTYLE

People all over the world keep geckos as pets. Pet owners might keep many females and one male gecko together. Males stress each other out. They should not be kept together.

GECKO SOCIETY FACT

Most geckos eat their skin after shedding it.

NOISY GECKOS

Geckos are the most vocal of all lizards.

Gecko Society

Geckos like to live alone. When they are ready to mate, they must find each other. They produce scents called pheromones. These scents attract mates.

Geckos communicate by making sounds. They call to mates. They warn their neighbors of danger. Stressed geckos may scream. Relaxed geckos sometimes chirp. Geckos also bark, trill, click, and yelp!

Male geckos become aggressive toward each other when they are looking for mates. They stiffen their bodies and raise their tails. This is called posturing. It makes them look bigger. Posturing males hiss or scream until one backs down and leaves.

XEMPLARY SKILLS FACT

Geckos can run straight up a wall at more than three feet (0.9 m) per second.

XEMPLARY SKILLS

Geckos have extreme features. Large eyes help them find food in dim light. Clinging toe pads help them climb quickly. But some have feet suited to other purposes.

When a gecko falls, it twists its tail sharply to one side. This allows it to land on its feet.

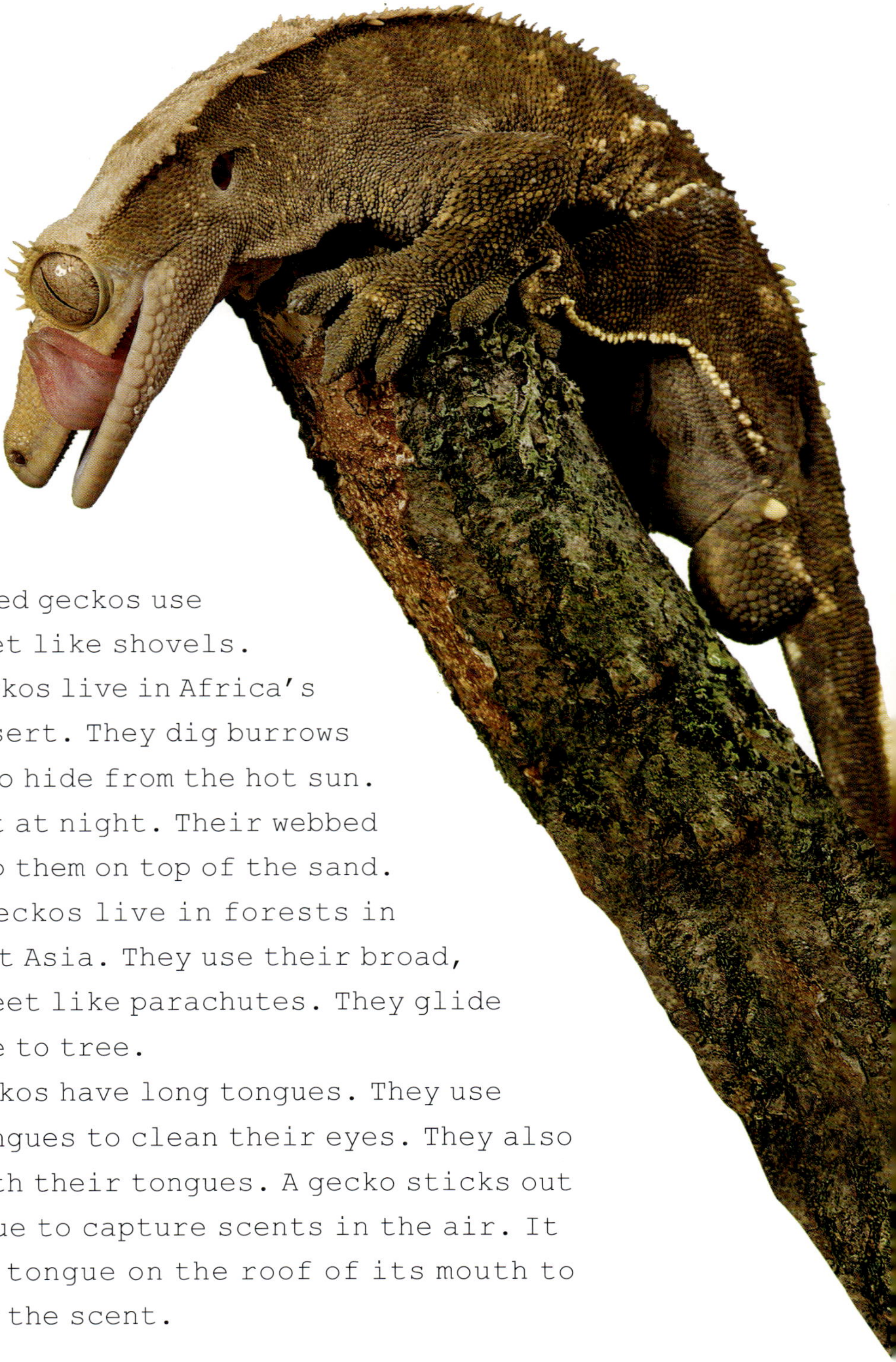

Web-footed geckos use their feet like shovels. These geckos live in Africa's Namib Desert. They dig burrows in sand to hide from the hot sun. They hunt at night. Their webbed feet keep them on top of the sand. Flying geckos live in forests in Southeast Asia. They use their broad, webbed feet like parachutes. They glide from tree to tree.

Geckos have long tongues. They use their tongues to clean their eyes. They also smell with their tongues. A gecko sticks out its tongue to capture scents in the air. It rubs its tongue on the roof of its mouth to identify the scent.

TOP FIVE XTREME GECKOS

3

Xtreme Gecko #3

Leopard Longevity The oldest gecko in the world lived nearly 32 years. A former reptile scientist named Ron Tremper hatched the leopard gecko in 1981. Tremper also hatched a female leopard gecko that lived for more than 21 years! In the wild, these geckos live six to eight years. This is a long time for such small lizards. Some scientists believe **brumation** helps these reptiles live longer.

XASPERATING CONFLICT

In Costa Rica and Southeast Asia, geckos are symbols of good luck. But in parts of Africa, geckos are said to bring misfortune.

Gecko Survival

Around the world, humans push geckos out of their natural homes to make way for cities and farms. In some places, geckos are taken from the wild. They are used in folk medicine. Or they are sold as pets.

Gecko bodies are covered in colors and patterns. These markings match their surroundings. This helps geckos hide from predators. Hungry birds, rodents, and snakes eat geckos.

A gecko can separate its tail from its body. If the gecko feels very threatened, its tail simply drops off and wiggles! Predators focus on the moving tail. The gecko runs away! Most gecko tails grow back.

GECKO LIFESPAN

Wild	up to 12 years
Captive	more than 20 years →

Some geckos live in places with cold winters. Western banded geckos and leopard geckos become sluggish. Their body functions slow down. They do not eat. This is called brumation. It lasts five to eight months. As temperatures rise, the geckos become more active. They begin searching for food.

GECKO SURVIVAL FACT

Some geckos store extra fat in their tails.

Geckos rely on this fat during brumation.

TOP FIVE XTREME GECKOS

Xtreme Gecko #2

Lost and Found In 1993, the New Caledonian crested gecko was declared **extinct**. It had not been seen in 100 years. The next year, a tropical storm passed through New Caledonia. It forced many animals out of flooded forests. Scientists rediscovered the crested gecko in three separate locations! Today, one group lives on the Isle of Pines. Two groups live on New Caledonia's main island, Grande Terre. This gecko is now protected.

XCITING FACTS

The Mediterranean gecko was brought to Florida in 1910. It is now commonly seen there.

Monito geckos were nearly wiped out by rats on Puerto Rico's Monito Island.

Each of a gecko's feet has up to 1.6 million setae!

Flying geckos can glide as far as 200 feet (61 m) between trees.

A cat gecko curls up with its tail around its face to sleep—just like a cat.

Large geckos may eat small snakes, birds, and rodents.

Geckos' eyes are 350 times more sensitive to light than humans'.

Bavay's gecko can give off a skunk-like smell to scare away predators.

Leopard geckos are unique. They have eyelids, and they do not have gripping toe pads.

Crested geckos cannot regrow their tails.

The psychedelic rock gecko has a purple body, yellow head, and orange limbs.

Leaf-tailed geckos (pictured) have broad flat tails that are larger than their heads.

Geckos in New Zealand typically give birth to twins.

Geckos are not covered in rough scales. The soft bumps

on a gecko's skin are called tubercles.

TOP FIVE XTREME GECKOS

1

Xtreme Gecko #1

Smallest Reptiles The Jaragua dwarf gecko and the Virgin Islands dwarf gecko (pictured) are among the smallest reptiles on Earth. These geckos are about the length of a kidney bean. The Jaragua dwarf gecko lives in the rainforests of Beata Island in the Dominican Republic. The Virgin Islands dwarf gecko has been found on only 3 of the more than 50 British Virgin Islands.

GLOSSARY

brumation – a period of inactivity when reptiles slow down their breathing and heart rate

extinct – having no living members

nocturnal – active at night

parasites – animals or plants that live on or inside another living thing (called a host) while giving nothing back to the host; some parasites cause disease or even death

particles – very small parts of matter

reptiles – animals with dry, scaly skin whose body temperatures change with their surroundings

RESOURCES

"The Amazing Gecko: 20 Interesting Facts about the World's Most Species-Rich Lizard. The Ark in Space. http://www.arkinspace.com/2013/07/gecko-20-interesting-facts-about-worlds.html.

De Vosjoli, Philippe. *Crested Geckos*. Irvine, Calif.: Lumina, 2014.

"Gecko." National Geographic Kids. http://kids.nationalgeographic.com/animals/gecko/#gecko-on-leaf.jpg.

Marsico, Katie. *Geckos*. Danbury, Conn.: Children's Press, 2013.

INDEX

Geckos cannot swim, but they do not mind rain.